INTO THE WIND

SAILBOATS THEN AND NOW

D1716280

INTO THE WIND

SAILBOATS THEN AND NOW

Steve Otfinoski

MARSHALL CAVENDISH
NEW YORK

Benchmark Books
Marshall Cavendish Corporation
99 White Plains Road
Tarrytown, New York 10591-9001

Library of Congress-in-Publication Data
Otfinoski, Steven.
Into the wind : sailboats then and now / by Steven Otfinoski.
   p.   cm. — (Here we go!)
Includes bibliographical references and index.
Summary: Examines the history of sailboats and describes different kinds
that are used today.
ISBN 0-7614-0405-8 (lb)
1. Sailboats—Juvenile literature. [1. Sailboats. 2. Boats and boating.]
I.Title II.Series: Here we go! (New York, N.Y.)
VM150.085   1997   623.8'203—dc20   96-18479   CIP   AC

Photo research by Ellen Barrett Dudley

Cover photo: *The Image Bank,* Eric Schweikardt

The photographs in this book are used by permission and through the
courtesy of: *The Image Bank:* Marcel Isy Schwart, 1, 19 (bottom); Robbi
Newman, 2; HMS Images, 6; J.L Stage, 8 (left); Jacques Cochin, 15; Guido
Alberto Rossi, 16–17, 29; Jay Freis, 17; William Kennedy, 19 (top); Zanon
Gianfranco, 20; Place, 21; Michael Garff, 22 (left); Nicholas Foster, 23 (left);
Michael Melford, 23 (right); Gerard Champlong, 25; Rentmeester, 26
(bottom); Alvis Upitis, 27; Nicholas Foster, back cover. *Photo Researchers:*
Bud Lehnhausen, 7; Archiv, 8 (right), 9 (top and bottom); Gianni Tortoli,
10; Cossec/Explorer, 11, 18; Joe Sohm, 12; Farrell Grehan, 13; David E.
Edgerton, 16; Jim Corwin, 22 (right); Plisson/Explorer, 24; Petit-Wind, 26
(top); John Clare du Bois, 30; Ulrike Welsch, 32. *Peter Arnold:* James H.
Karales, 28.

Printed in the United States of America

6   5   4   3   2   1

To Dad,

the intrepid skipper of the <u>Hi Ho</u>

*H*ave you ever set a toy sailboat
down on a pond and then watched
as the wind carried it across the water?
The thrill of sailing is unlike
any other experience.
It all began when an early human
put the first sail on a hollowed–out log.
People's love affair with sailboats has
been going strong ever since.

Oceanica Classis

Sturdy longboats (above left) carried the Vikings
up and down the coast of Europe and even
across the Atlantic Ocean to America.
The dragon's head in the prow was meant
to frighten their enemies.
Nearly five hundred years after the Vikings, Christopher
Columbus sailed to America in the *Santa Maria* (above right).

Europeans explored new lands and traded with different peoples in their sailing ships. Marco Polo visited China in the 1200s in this ship (top). Ferdinand Magellan's ship *Victoria* (bottom) was the first to go around the world in 1522.

Over the next two hundred years,
sailing ships grew larger and more luxurious.
Spanish galleons carried gold, spices, and other
treasures from the New World back to Spain.
This copy of the galleon *Neptune* (left) has a
towering statue of the sea god on its prow.
Tall ships, like the two above, defended themselves
and their cargo from other ships with cannons.

The *Mayflower* carried neither gold nor cannon, but it brought the first Pilgrims to America in 1620. The *Mayflower II* was built in the 1950s. It crossed the Atlantic Ocean from England to America in fifty–four days. That's eleven days less than it took the first *Mayflower* to make the same voyage.

By the mid–1800s, a new kind of ship ruled the seas.

Clipper ships were so named because they were fast and "clipped off" the miles.

They had enormous sails and streamlined bodies.

Clipper ships carried thousands of adventurers to the gold fields of California and Australia.

Many clippers crossed the Atlantic in just twelve days.

Then new ships powered by steam were invented.

They didn't have to rely on the wind to move them.

By 1900, the days of the great sailing ships were over.

Today, sailboats in America are used for racing and recreation.
But in many parts of the world they still have other uses.
This tall, accordian–like sail (left) rises from a Chinese
fishing boat.
The boat in the middle is called a "junk." But it's not at all "junky."
It is well made with strong sails of cotton cloth.
This junk is a houseboat for a family and its animals.
The outrigger (right) of Indonesia has a wooden framework
that helps keep it from capsizing in rough waters.

At sea, each sail must be trimmed, or set at an angle, to catch the wind and keep the boat moving in the right direction.
It takes all a sailor's skill and strength to pull on the ropes that are tied to the bottom of the sails.
On a boat, ropes are called lines and the bottom of the sail is its foot. When you become a sailor, you have to learn a whole new language!

The bigger the boat, the more sails it needs to pick up speed. The larger South American boat has three sails. The smaller fishing boat—a *jangada*—from Brazil needs only one.

Sails do more than catch the wind.

The sails on these Italian boats are like colorful flags that identify their owners.

The bright, balloon–shaped sails (right) are called spinnakers.

When a spinnaker is set and a stiff breeze is up, a sailboat can seem to fly with the wind.

Small sailboats can go almost anywhere there is water—
from the bustle of New York Harbor to the still beauty
of a mountain lake.

Sailboats come in all shapes and sizes,
from a tiny catboat (left) to this large schooner (right)
racing off the coast of Maine.

Sailboat racing is an exciting sport—
for both adults and children.
Teamwork is everything in a big race.
The crew must work together like the parts of a machine.
Sails are raised and lowered in a snap as soon as the skipper
gives the command.

Every second counts as the skippers strive to gain
a foot or two and burst ahead over the finish line.

There are other kinds of sailing for those who love adventure. Windsurfing (above left) is a wild blend of surfing and sailing. The daredevil below is desert board sailing on a beach in Morocco. Who says you can't sail when the water freezes? This hardy soul is sailing an iceboat on New York's frozen Hudson River at night.

There is nothing quite like the feel of a sailboat
as it heads into the wind.
All you need is a steady breeze, a good sail,
and a spirit of adventure.
At the helm of a sailboat, we are all
Christopher Columbus, setting off into the unknown,
wherever the wind will take us!

FIND OUT MORE

Bailey, Donna. *Sailing.* Austin, TX: Raintree Steck–Vaughn, 1990.

Chant, Chris. *Sailing Ships.* Tarrytown, New York: Marshall Cavendish, 1990.

Crews, Donald. *Sail Away.* New York: Greenwillow, 1995.

Evans, Jeremy. *Sailing.* New York: Macmillan, 1992.

INDEX

STEVE OTFINOSKI has written more than sixty books for children. He also has a theater company called *History Alive!* that performs plays for schools about people and events from the past. Steve lives in Stratford, Connecticut, with his wife and two children.